D1611079

the publisher will be corrected in future editions.

This publication is a creative work fully protected
by all applicable copyright laws, as well as by
misappropriation trade secret unfair competition,

Copyright © 1997

Gale Research
835 Penobscot Building
645 Griswold St.
Detroit, Ml 48226-4094

ISBN 0-7876-1687-7
ISSN 1094-3552

Printed in the United States of America
10 9 8 7 6 5 4

Wuthering Heights

Emily Brontë

1847

Introduction

First published in 1847, Emily Brontë's *Wuthering Heights* ranks high on the list of major works of English literature. A brooding tale of passion and revenge set in the Yorkshire moors, the novel has inspired no fewer than four film versions in modern times. Early critics did not like the work, citing its excess of passion and its coarseness. A second edition was published in 1850, two years after the author's death. Sympathetically prefaced by her sister Charlotte, it met with greater success, and the novel has continued to grow in stature ever since. In the novel a pair of narrators, Mr. Lockwood and Nelly Dean, relate the story of the foundling Heathcliff's arrival at Wuthering Heights, and the close-knit bond he forms with his benefactor's daughter, Catherine Earnshaw. One in spirit, they are nonetheless social unequals, and the saga of frustrated yearning and destruction that follows Catherine's refusal to marry Heathcliff is unique in the English canon. The novel is admired not least for the power of its imagery, its complex structure, and its ambiguity, the very elements that confounded its first critics. Emily Brontë spent her short life mostly at home, and apart from her own fertile imagination, she drew her inspiration from the local landscape—the surrounding moorlands and the regional architecture of the Yorkshire area —as well as her personal experience of religion, of folklore, and of illness and death. Dealing with themes of nature, cruelty, social position, and indestructibility of the spirit, *Wuthering Heights* has surpassed the more successful Charlotte Brontë's *Jane Eyre* in academic and popular circles.

Author Biography

Emily Jane Brontë was born on July 30, 1818, to Maria Branwell and the Reverend Patrick Brontë, in Thornton, Yorkshire, England. She was the fifth of six children, and the fourth daughter. The family moved to a parsonage in Haworth in 1820, and following the death of Maria Brontë in 1821, the children's maternal aunt came to care for them. In 1825 Emily was sent to join her sisters Maria, Elizabeth, and Charlotte at school, but after an epidemic at the school claimed the lives of Maria and Elizabeth, Emily and Charlotte returned home. Emily would remain at home for the next ten years. In 1826 Patrick Brontë gave his children a set of toy soldiers, and the children began to make up stories about them. A realm in Africa, called Angria, was largely the inspiration of Charlotte and brother Branwell, but soon Emily and Anne had invented the Pacific Island of Gondal, which would figure in poems and stories they wrote throughout their lives. Emily was uncomfortable with outsiders and made only brief, intermittent attempts to construct a life for herself away from the parsonage. An unsuccessful experiment as Charlotte's pupil in East Yorkshire that began in 1835 ended after a year. She was similarly ill-suited for a position as assistant teacher at Law Hill School near Halifax. In 1842, Charlotte and Emily traveled to Brussels, Belgium, intending to study languages, but returned home later that year because of the death of their aunt, who had left them what money she had.

In 1845 Charlotte discovered a private notebook of Emily's poems and persuaded her to publish a selection of them. Emily reluctantly agreed, and a volume of poetry that included "Remembrance," "The Prisoner," "The Philosopher," and "Stars" appeared in 1846. It sold only two copies, but one critic was flattering. *Wuthering Heights* appeared in 1847 under the pseudonym Ellis Bell and was panned by contemporary critics, who objected to its coarseness and brutality. In contrast, Charlotte's novel *Jane Eyre*, published the same year, was a runaway success. Emily produced one further poem in 1846; *Wuthering Heights* was her only novel. In 1848 Branwell Brontë died, in part owing to his dissolute ways, which were a source of constant concern to his sisters. Emily caught cold at his funeral and developed tuberculosis. Refusing to seek medical treatment, she died on December 19, 1848.

The lack of biographical material about Emily Brontë makes her an enigmatic figure and her work difficult to evaluate. The poems, in particular, suffer from a lack of context, and ambiguous punctuation. Although the poems are often clumsy, they show flashes of the same originality that makes *Wuthering Heights* so compelling. Emily Brontë did not know success during her lifetime, but despite the initial failure of *Wuthering Heights*, she has proved a giant among writers.

Plot Summary

Part I—Childhood

Set on the Yorkshire moors of England, *Wuthering Heights* opens with the comments of Mr. Lockwood, the newly arrived tenant of Thrushcross Grange. He tells of his visit to Wuthering Heights, where he encounters his landlord and neighbor, Mr. Heathcliff; Joseph, Heathcliff's pious and surly old servant; Hareton Earnshaw, an ignorant and impoverished young man; and the beautiful Catherine Heathcliff, widow of Heathcliff's dead son. Rough weather forces Lockwood to spend the night. He finds several old books, the margins of which had been used as a childhood diary by Catherine Earnshaw, mother to the current Catherine. Perusing these pages, Lockwood learns about the childhood adventures of Heathcliff and the first Catherine, and of their oppression by Catherine's brother, Hindley. Lockwood falls into a restless sleep, punctuated by nightmares in which the first Catherine Earnshaw comes to the bedroom window and begs to be let in. He awakes screaming, and in so doing he wakes Heathcliff, who opens the window and begs Catherine to come again. At sunrise Heathcliff escorts Lockwood back to Thrushcross Grange.

The next day, Lockwood, finding himself sick, persuades the servant, Nelly Dean, to sit and talk with him. She relates how she grew up at Wuthering Heights, and she tells how one night Mr. Earnshaw brought home the mysterious boy, Heathcliff, whom he had found starving in Liverpool. Mr. Earnshaw favors Heathcliff, causing his son Hindley to hate the interloper, but Heathcliff and the first Catherine become fast friends. Hindley is sent off to college, but after Mr. Earnshaw's death he returns with a wife and becomes master of Wuthering Heights. Under Hindley's tyranny, Catherine and Heathcliff grow closer and more mischievous, their favorite pastime being to wander the moors. On one such excursion they are caught looking in the windows of Thrushcross Grange, and Catherine is bitten by a bulldog and has to stay at the Grange for five weeks. Hindley, meanwhile, forbids Heathcliff to have further contact with Catherine.

Catherine returns much changed. She now dresses and acts like a lady, and she has befriended Edgar and Isabella Linton, the siblings who live at the Grange. Heathcliff feels her neglect sharply, and Catherine feels torn between loyalty to her old friend and attraction to her new companions. Hindley's new wife, Frances, gives birth to a son, Hareton, and dies of consumption, and Hindley starts drinking and becomes even more tyrannical. Heathcliff is deprived of all education and is forced to labor as one of the servants of the Heights. When Edgar proposes to Catherine, she accepts, but tells Nelly that she would never have done so if her brother had not turned Heathcliff into someone it would disgrace her to marry. Heathcliff overhears this comment and flees Wuthering Heights before she goes on to explain to Nelly the depth of her feelings for Heathcliff:

> "I cannot express it; but surely you and everybody have a notion that there is, or should be an existence of yours beyond you. What were the use of my creation if I were entirely contained here? My great miseries in this world have been Heathcliff's miseries, and I watched and felt each from the beginning; my great thought in living is himself. If all else perished, and *he* remained, I should still continue to be; and, if all else remained, and he were annihilated, the Universe would turn to a mighty stranger. I should not seem a part of it. My love for Linton is like the foliage in the woods. Time will change it, I am well aware, as winter changes the trees—my love for Heathcliff resembles the eternal rocks beneath—a source of little visible delight, but necessary. Nelly, I *am* Heathcliff—he is always, always in my mind—not as a pleasure, any more than I am always a pleasure to myself—but as my own being—so, do not talk of our separation again."

Part II—Marriage and Death

Catherine and Edgar are married and seem happy, until Heathcliff returns, mysteriously wealthy and educated. He takes up residence at Wuthering Heights, where he gambles Hindley out of all his possessions. Heathcliff quickly resumes his acquaintance with Catherine, to her delight and Edgar's annoyance. Isabella, Edgar's sister, begins to love Heathcliff, in spite of repeated warnings about his character. Heathcliff, desiring Isabella's inheritance, begins to encourage the attraction, and when Nelly informs Edgar of this courtship he becomes enraged. A fight ensues between Edgar and Heathcliff, and Heathcliff is banished from the Grange. Catherine, to punish Edgar, refuses to eat for three days and drives herself into a feverish delirium. While Edgar is nursing her back to a fragile state of health, Isabella and Heathcliff elope. Isabella soon regrets her marriage to the cruel Heathcliff. She writes to Nelly, telling her of her miserable life at Wuthering Heights and begging her to visit. Heathcliff takes advantage of Nelly's visit to request a meeting with Catherine, who is pregnant. Nelly reluctantly agrees, and a few days later, while Edgar is at church, Heathcliff enters the Grange and sees Catherine for the last time. Edgar enters and finds Heathcliff embracing Catherine, who has fainted. Catherine dies without ever fully regaining her senses, although two hours before her death, she gives birth to a daughter. Edgar and Heathcliff are both distraught at Catherine's death, and Heathcliff begs her ghost to haunt him.

Days after Catherine's death, Isabella appears at the Grange, having fled the Heights. She swears she will not return, but she refuses to stay at the Grange because she fears Heathcliff will find her there. She moves to the South of England and gives birth to a sickly boy she names Linton.

Part III—The Second Generation

Shortly after Isabella's escape, the doctor, Kenneth, brings news of Hindley's death. Nelly wants Edgar to take in Hindley's son Hareton, but Heathcliff vows that if they take Hareton from him he will take his child from Isabella. He asserts that he wants to see if the same mistreatment will affect Hindley's child as Hindley's abuse affected Heathcliff.

Twelve years later, Isabella, near death, writes to her brother and asks him to care for her son after her death. Edgar brings Linton home, but Heathcliff immediately demands custody of his son. He reveals to Nelly his plan to see his child ruling over both Thrushcross Grange and Wuthering Heights.

Young Catherine, daughter of Catherine and Edgar, is not told that her cousin is so close by, but one day on a walk on the moor, she meets Heathcliff and Hareton and is reacquainted with Linton. Heathcliff tells Nelly that he hopes Linton and young Catherine will fall in love and marry. He boasts about how he has turned Hareton, a naturally intelligent boy, into an ignorant brute, while raising his own weak and selfish son up as Hareton's master. When Edgar hears of his daughter's visit, he does his best to impress on her the evil nature of

Heathcliff and the importance of avoiding the Heights. Catherine nevertheless commences a secret correspondence with Linton, which only ends when Nelly discovers the love letters and threatens to tell Catherine's father. Heathcliff, however, convinces Catherine that Linton is dying of grief because of their broken correspondence, and Nelly reluctantly agrees to accompany Catherine on a visit to the Heights. That visit leads to a series of clandestine visits by young Catherine to the Heights. Edgar puts a stop to the visits, but finally agrees to let Catherine and Linton meet for weekly strolls on the moor. During the second of these excursions, Heathcliff, knowing that Edgar is near death, tricks Catherine and Nelly into entering Wuthering Heights, where he imprisons them and forces Catherine to marry Linton. Catherine convinces Linton to help her escape, and she arrives at the Grange just in time to see her dying father. During her absence from the Heights, Heathcliff forces Linton to make Heathcliff the inheritor of all of his and Catherine's property. After her father's death, young Catherine is forced to return to the Heights and tend to her dying husband. He dies shortly after her arrival, and Catherine, impoverished and alone, is forced to stay on at the Heights.

The day after hearing this story, Lockwood visits the Heights and gives notice that he will be leaving for London. Returning months later to settle some business, he finds Thrushcross Grange deserted and matters much changed at the Heights. Hareton and Catherine, previously sworn enemies, have fallen in love, and Catherine is aiding Hareton in his attempts to educate himself. Nelly is now employed at the Heights, and while the lovers enjoy a walk on the moor, Nelly informs Lockwood of Heathcliff's death, which followed four days of starvation during which he was haunted by the vision of his beloved Catherine. He was buried, as requested, next to Catherine, with the adjoining sides of the two coffins removed so that their ashes could mingle, and the country folks claim that a person walking on the moors will sometimes see the ghosts of Heathcliff and Catherine wandering their old playground.

Ellen Dean

One of the novel's two narrators, Nelly is loyal but conventional, and reads very little into events. In his introduction to *Wuthering Heights*, David Daiches remarks on the contrast between the tone of the narrative and the high drama of the goingson of the story: "It is to what might be called the sublime deadpan of the telling that the extraordinary force of the novel can largely be attributed…. At no point does Nelly throw up her hands and exclaim: 'For God's sake, what is going on here? What kind of people *are* they?'" For instance, after Heathcliff has spent the night in the Linton's garden bashing his head against a tree trunk, Nelly notices "several splashes of blood about the bark of the tree, and his hands and forehead were both stained; probably the scene I witnessed was a repetition of others acted during the night. It hardly moved my compassion— it appalled me; still I felt reluctant to quit him so." Nelly's familiarity with the actors is an important element of the narration, and a hazard of her station is that she must repeatedly be the bearer of news that will move the action in a fateful direction. On the eve of Heathcliff's return, for example, Edgar and the first Catherine look "wonderfully peaceful," and Nelly shrinks from having to announce Heathcliff, though duty compels her to, just as she shrinks later from having to tell Heathcliff of the first Catherine's death, but does. Nelly has a mind of her own, and she does not hesitate to query the first Catherine about her reasons for marrying Edgar, or to suggest to Heathcliff at the end of the novel that he might want to make his confession before dying. Nevertheless, the kind of passion that exists between Heathcliff and the first Catherine is far beyond her imagination.

Nelly Dean

See Ellen Dean

Catherine Earnshaw

Cathy Earnshaw is six when her father brings back with him from Liverpool not the whip she asked for but the seven-year-old foundling Heathcliff, who is soon her constant companion. Cathy is a "wild, wick slip," beautiful, and "much too fond of Heathcliff." Though capable of sweetness, she likes "to act the little mistress," and it is the awareness of the social differences between her and Heathcliff that lead her, despite her love for him, to marry Edgar Linton, whom she finds "handsome, and pleasant to be with." When Nelly implies that her reasons are superficial, Cathy tells of her plan to use Edgar's money to help Heathcliff to rise. "It would degrade me to marry Heathcliff, now," she tells Nelly, "so he shall never know how I love him"; yet "he's more myself than I am.… Nelly, I *am* Heathcliff." Five months after Cathy's marriage to Linton, during which time Nelly observes that the couple seem to be increasingly happy, Heathcliff returns, transformed. Their "mutual joy" at seeing each other again is undeniable, and from that point on Cathy lives with a painfully divided heart. She refuses to respond to Edgar's request that she choose between the two men. Although Heathcliff has the looks and manners of a gentleman, the revenge he plans is diabolical, and though she loves him, Cathy is not fooled. "He's a fierce, pitiless, wolfish man…: and he'd crush you, like a sparrow's egg," she tells an infatuated Isabella. When Cathy and Heathcliff meet for the last time, she tells him, "You and Edgar have broken my heart, Heathcliff! … I shall not be at peace." She dies two hours after midnight, having given birth to a "puny, seven months' child."

Cathy Earnshaw

See Catherine Earnshaw

Frances Earnshaw

Wife of Hindley. Dies after giving birth to Hareton.

Hareton Earnshaw

The son of Frances and Hindley Earnshaw, Hareton, too, is initially targeted by Heathcliff as an object of revenge, and is degraded by him. But Heathcliff develops a grudging affection for the boy, favoring him over his own weakling son,

Linton, and when Heathcliff dies, Hareton weeps over his body. Nelly sees him as "owning better qualities than his father ever possessed. Good things lost among a wilderness of weeds." Hareton is, however, transformed by his love for Catherine, who teaches him to read.

Hindley Earnshaw

Hindley Earnshaw, the first Catherine's brother, is fourteen when Heathcliff is brought to Wuthering Heights. Hindley hates and envies him because Mr. Earnshaw clearly favors the new boy. Hindley continually degrades Heathcliff, a habit that intensifies after the death of Mr. Earnshaw. After the death of his beloved wife Frances, Hindley resorts to drinking and gambling, and neglects both his sister Catherine and his son Hareton. Upon Heathcliff's return to Wuthering Heights after a three-year absence, five months after Edgar Linton and the first Catherine have married, Hindley befriends Heathcliff in the hopes of winning money from him. Blaming Hindley for the loss of the first Catherine, Heathcliff ruthlessly encourages Hindley to drink and eventually wins Wuthering Heights from him. After Hindley dies, Heathcliff brutalizes Hareton, though he eventually abandons the attempt after the second Catherine Linton and Hareton fall in love.

Mr. Earnshaw

Father of Hindley and the first Catherine. He

brings Heathcliff home into the family. He was strict with his children.

Mrs. Earnshaw

Mother of Hindley and the first Catherine. She didn't protest the mistreatment of Heathcliff and died two years after he joined the Earnshaw household.

Heathcliff

On his return from a business trip to Liverpool, Mr. Earnshaw brings with him "a dirty, ragged, black-haired" orphan from a Liverpool slum. The boy, seven-year-old Heathcliff, and the first Catherine Earnshaw are almost immediately inseparable. Hindley Earnshaw, however, is jealous of Mr. Earnshaw's obvious preference for Heathcliff, and he abuses him. Heathcliff returns the hatred. "From the very beginning he bred bad feeling in the house," says Nelly Dean, one of the two narrators of *Wuthering Heights*, about the force that has entered their lives. Heathcliff knows only two loyalties, to the first Cathy and to Mr. Earnshaw, and at Earnshaw's death he and Cathy "both set up a heart-breaking cry." He tries to control his jealousy over Cathy's growing friendship with Edgar Linton for her sake—"Nelly, make me decent, I'm going to be good." But later, overhearing a conversation in which Cathy says it would degrade her to marry him, he steals away and does not return to Wuthering Heights until five months after Cathy has married Edgar Linton.

Media Adaptations

- *Wuthering Heights* continues to inspire filmmakers: adaptations include those by William Wyler, starring Laurence Olivier and Merle Oberon, 1939, available from HBO Home Video and Home Vision Cinema; by Robert Fuest, starring Timothy Dalton and Anna Calder-Marshall, 1970, available from Congress Entertainment, Karol Video, The Video Catalog; a reworking under the title "Abismos de pasion", by Luis Buñuel, starring Jorge Mistral and Irasema Dilian, 1953, available from Xenon, Media Home Entertainment, Applause Productions; and by Peter

Kosminsky, starring Ralph Fiennes and Juliette Binoche, 1992 (not released in the U.S., but later broadcast on Turner Network Television).

- Sound recordings have been published by Listen for Pleasure, 1981; Recorded Books, 1981, and Bantam Doubleday Dell Audio, 1995. The novel was read by Michael Page and Laurel Merlington for an audio version, Brilliance Corporation, 1992, entitled *Wuthering Heights Readalong*, Lake Publishing Co., 1994.

- The novel has been adapted as a four-act opera by Bernard Herrman, libretto by Lucille Fletcher, 1950. An adaptation by Carlisle Floyd, who also wrote the libretto, in three acts was first performed in 1958. The novel was also adapted for the stage by Charles Vance and published by Samuel French, 1990.

Heathcliff is transformed on his return—"tall, athletic, well-formed"—but he is hell-bent on avenging the loss of Cathy, and he sets about destroying the inhabitants of both Wuthering Heights and Thrushcross Grange with a fury. His assertion of what David Daiches, in his introduction to *Wuthering Heights*, calls Heathcliff's "natural claims" to Cathy "over the artificial claim of her husband" is welcomed by Cathy, though the strain eventually kills her. Heathcliff cruelly exploits Hindley, Isabella, Hareton, the second Catherine, and Linton, his own son. "I have no pity," he tells Nelly. Yet when the first Catherine dies, he is inconsolable, bashing his head repeatedly against a tree trunk: "I *cannot* live without my life! I *cannot* live without my soul!" And he has an obvious affection for Hareton, despite his determination to degrade the boy. Heathcliff is largely incomprehensible to those around him, seemingly human and inhuman, a walking contradiction. "Is Mr. Heathcliff a man?" Isabella writes to Nelly, following her marriage to him, "If so, is he mad? And if not, is he a devil?" Toward the end of the novel Heathcliff confesses to Nelly that he no longer cares for revenge: "I have lost the faculty of enjoying their destruction." As determined to join his "immortal love" as he once was to ruin his enemies, he tells Nelly that he feels "a strange change coming," and, forgetting to eat, starves himself. Even death, however, does not compose his features, and Joseph remarks that he looks as though the devil has carried him off.

Catherine Heathcliff

See Catherine Linton

Isabella Heathcliff

See Isabella Linton

Linton Heathcliff

Linton Heathcliff is the spoiled, weakling son of Isabella and Heathcliff. He is forced by Heathcliff to marry the second Catherine Linton to secure for Heathcliff, at Linton's death, Thrushcross Grange. Nobody except the second Catherine Linton likes Linton very much; the housekeeper at the Heights complains to Nelly that he is "a fainthearted creature" who can't bear to have the window open at night. His character serves the dual purpose of providing a mechanism whereby Heathcliff can acquire Thrushcross Grange and re-create the Edgar-Cathy-Heathcliff triangle of the previous generation. Linton dies soon after his marriage to the second Catherine.

Joseph

Joseph is the curmudgeonly, judgmental long-time servant at Wuthering Heights. He believes in eternal damnation and the likelihood of everyone he knows being bound for it, and he scolds constantly in a sometimes difficult-to-follow Yorkshire accent. As in the case of the narrators of the novel, Joseph's authenticity anchors the wilder elements of the story. Winifred Gerin observes in *Reference Guide to English Literature* that "in creating such a character as Joseph, Emily Brontë showed that, undoubted visionary as she was, she also had her feet firmly planted on earth."

Catherine Linton

Catherine Linton is the daughter of Cathy and Edgar, beautiful, like her mother, but cooler. "Her anger was never furious, her love never fierce," Nelly remarks about her. Although forced by Heathcliff to marry Linton Heathcliff, she genuinely seems to care for her cousin. She is obviously less a force than her mother, but spirited nonetheless, and refuses to be cowed by Heathcliff: "You *are* miserable, are you not? Lonely, like the devil, and envious like him? *Nobody* loves you—*nobody* will cry for you, when you die! I wouldn't be you!" Although Catherine is at first put off by Hareton's loutishness, the sheer bleakness of their existence propels them toward each other, and she teaches him to read. They fall in love, and the understanding at the end of the novel is that they will marry and go to live at Thrushcross Grange.

Catherine Earnshaw Linton

See Catherine Earnshaw

Cathy Linton

See Catherine Linton

Edgar Linton

Edgar Linton is all the things Heathcliff is not: handsome, refined, kind, and patient, although the first Cathy later describes Edgar and his sister

Isabella as "spoiled children, [who] fancy the world was made for their accommodation." When Heathcliff says he wishes he had Edgar's looks and breeding, Nelly retorts: "And cried for Mamma at every turn, and trembled if a country lad heaved his fist against you, and sat at home all day for a shower of rain." On the other hand, Nelly observes that the first Cathy's spells of bad humor are "respected with sympathizing silence by her husband," and that Edgar has a "deep-rooted fear of ruffling her humor." Linton loves his wife genuinely, but he is ineffectual. Unable to get her to choose between himself and Heathcliff, he retreats to his library, oblivious to her distress until alerted to it by Nelly. After his wife dies, Edgar sits all night beside her body. Taking the measure of both Edgar and Hindley, Nelly remarks that Linton "displayed the true courage of a loyal and faithful soul: he trusted God; and God comforted him." Hindley, with the stronger head, proved the worse and weaker man.

Isabella Linton

Like her brother Edgar, Isabella is perceived by the inhabitants of Wuthering Heights as spoiled. Having glimpsed them through a window quarreling amid the splendor of Thrushcross Grange, Heathcliff tells Nelly, "We laughed outright at the petted things, we did despise them!" Nelly observes that Isabella is "infantile in manners, though possessed of keen wit, keen feelings, and a keen temper, too, if irritated." On Heathcliff's return to

Wuthering Heights after the first Cathy's marriage to Edgar, Isabella becomes infatuated with him, despite Cathy's warning that he "couldn't love a Linton." At first indifferent, Heathcliff responds when he realizes he might gain control of her property through marriage. Once she is committed to him, he cruelly mistreats her. Despite the abuse, Isabella refuses to help Hindley in his attempt to murder Heathcliff, though she has enough of a sense of self-preservation to escape back to Thrushcross Grange, where she crushes her wedding ring with a poker. "I can recollect yet how I loved him," she tells Nelly, "and can dimly imagine that I could still be loving him, if—." Pregnant, Isabella flees to London, where she bears Linton. She dies when Linton is twelve, after which the boy comes to live with Heathcliff at the Heights.

Mr. Linton

Father of Edgar and Isabella. He is the owner of Thrushcross Grange.

Mrs. Linton

Mother of Edgar and Isabella. She takes the first Catherine in for a short while and exposed her to fine clothes and social behavior.

Mr. Lockwood

The other narrator of *Wuthering Heights*, Mr. Lockwood is, like Nelly Dean, conventional. But he lacks Nelly's perception, and appears even a little foolish. At first he judges Heathcliff to be a "capital fellow," and later he fantasizes a liaison with the second Catherine Linton. Several critics have remarked on his name as hinting at a "locked or closed mind." In his introduction to *Wuthering Heights*, David Daiches describes his general timidity: "he had aroused the love of 'a fascinating creature,' but retreated in panic when he realized it." Mr. Lockwood foreshadows the theme of cruelty that pervades the novel, rubbing the wrist of the ghost of the first Catherine Linton across a broken pane of glass in an attempt to loosen her grasp of his hand. Mr. Lockwood serves to vary the narrative perspective of the novel; his view of events in the present contrasts with Nelly's retrospective view.

Zillah

A servant at Wuthering Heights.

Themes

Love and Passion

Passion, particularly unnatural passion, is a predominant theme of Wuthering Heights. The first Catherine's devotion to Heathcliff is immediate and absolute, though she will not marry him, because to do so would degrade her. "Whatever our souls are made of, his and mine are the same, and Linton's is as different as a moonbeam from lightning, or frost from fire." Although there has been at least one Freudian interpretation of the text, the nature of the passion between Catherine and Heathcliff does not appear to be based on sex. David Daiches writes, "Ultimate passion is for her rather a kind of recognition of one's self—one's true and absolute self—in the object of passion." Catherine's passion is contrasted to the coolness of Linton, whose "cold blood cannot be worked into a fever." When he retreats into his library, she explodes, "What in the name of all that feels, has he to do with *books*, when I am dying?"

Revenge

Heathcliff's devotion to Catherine, on the other hand, is ferocious, and when frustrated, he conceives a plan of revenge of enormous proportions. Catherine's brother Hindley shares her passionate nature, though he devotes most of his energies to degrading Heathcliff. In some respects the passion that Catherine and Heathcliff share is so pure that it approaches a kind of spirituality. "I cannot express it," says Catherine, "but surely you and everybody have a notion that there is, or should be an existence of yours beyond you." In the characters of Heathcliff and Hindley, who both feel slighted in love, Brontë draws a parallel between the need for love and the strength of revenge.

Violence and Cruelty

Closely tied to the theme of revenge, but sometimes independent of it, are themes of cruelty and sadism, which are a recurring motif throughout the novel. Cruelty can be manifested emotionally, as in Mr. Earnshaw's disdain for his natural-born son, or in the first Catherine's apparent rejection of Heathcliff in favor of Edgar. The characters are given to physical cruelty as well. "Terror made me cruel," says Lockwood at the outset of the story, and proceeds to rub the wrists of the ghost Catherine against a broken windowpane in an effort to free himself from her grasp. Hindley torments Heathcliff, as Heathcliff will later torment Hareton. And although he has no affection for her, Heathcliff marries Isabella and then treats her so badly that she asks Nelly whether he is a devil. Sadism is also a recurring thematic element. Heathcliff tries to strangle Isabella's dog, and Hareton hangs a litter of puppies from the back of a chair. The first Catherine's early refusal of Heathcliff has elements of masochism (self-abuse) in it, as does her letting him back into her life, since her divided heart will eventually kill her.

Class Conflict

To the characters of Wuthering Heights, property ownership and social standing are inextricable. The Earnshaws and the Lintons both own estates, whereas Heathcliff is a foundling and has nothing. The first Catherine plans to marry Linton to use her husband's money to raise Heathcliff's social standing, thus freeing him from Hindley's domination. Her plan is foiled when Heathcliff disappears after hearing Catherine say that to marry him would degrade her. When he returns, he exerts great efforts to do people out of their property: first Hindley, then Isabella, then the second Catherine Linton. He takes revenge on Hareton by ensuring that the boy is raised in ignorance, with loutish manners, so that he will never escape his station. The story comes full cycle when Catherine Linton teaches Hareton to read, thus winning his love. The understanding at the end of the novel is that the couple will move to Thrushcross Grange.

Nature

"Wuthering" is a Yorkshire term for roaring of the wind, and themes of nature, both human and nonhuman, are closely associated with violence throughout the story. The local landscape is as storm-tossed as are the hearts of the inhabitants of

Wuthering Heights; cycles of births and deaths occur as relentlessly as the cycles of the seasons. The characters feel themselves so intrinsically a part of their environment that the first Catherine compares her love for Edgar to "foliage in the woods," and that for Heathcliff to "the eternal rocks beneath." In detailing his plan to debase Hareton, Heathcliff says, "We will see if one tree will not grow as crooked as another, with the same wind to twist it!" The novel opens with a snowstorm, and ends with the flowering of spring, mirroring the passions that fuel the drama and the peace that follows its resolution.

Topics for Further Study

- What achievements of modern medicine have reduced the high rates of maternal deaths in childbirth that were commonplace during the period of the novel? How have social factors compromised advances in the treatment of tuberculosis?

- What were the milestones in women's rights that have reduced the vulnerability of women like the second Catherine Linton to loss of property?

- Explore how people grieve their dead in various cultures around the world, and how these customs compare with Edgar's request in *Wuthering Heights* that Nelly "get mourning" for the second Catherine after Isabella's death.

Supernatural

There are many references in the novel to the supernatural, and even when the references seem fairly literal, the characters do not seem to think them odd. When Lockwood first arrives, he encounters the ghost of the first Catherine Linton, and his telling of the event to Heathcliff arouses not disbelief but a strange passion. The bond between the first Catherine and Heathcliff is itself superhuman, and after she dies, Heathcliff implores her spirit, "I pray one prayer—I repeat it till my tongue stiffens—Catherine Earnshaw, may you not rest, as long as I am living! You said I killed you— haunt me then!" At Edgar Linton's death, Heathcliff persuades the gravedigger to open Catherine's coffin, and later confesses to Nelly that he has been haunted by Catherine's spirit for eighteen years. At the end of the novel, after Heathcliff's death, Nelly reports to Lockwood a child's claim that he has seen Heathcliff and a woman walking on the moors.

Narration

The power of *Wuthering Heights* owes much to its complex narrative structure and to the ingenious device of having two conventional people relate a very unconventional tale. The story is organized as a narrative within a narrative, or what some critics call "Chinese boxes." Lockwood is used to open and end the novel in the present tense, first person ("I"). When he returns to Thrushcross Grange from his visit to Wuthering Heights sick and curious, Nelly cheerfully agrees to tell him about his neighbors. She picks up the narrative and continues it, also in the first person, almost until the end, with only brief interruptions by Lockwood. The critic David Daiches notes in his introduction of *Wuthering Heights* the "fascinating counterpoint" of "end retrospect and present impression," and that the strength of the story relies on Nelly's familiarity with the main characters.

Setting

The novel is set in the Yorkshire moors of England, even now a bleakly beautiful, sparsely populated area of high rolling grassy hills, few trees, and scattered rocky outcroppings or patches of heather. The lowlands between the hills are marshy. The weather is changeable and, because the area is so open, sometimes wild. The exposed location of Wuthering Heights high on the moors is contrasted with the sheltered calm of Thrushcross Grange, which is nestled in a soft valley. Both seats reflect the characters of those who inhabit them. The descriptions of both houses also reflect the influence of the local architecture at the time of Brontë's writing, which often incorporated a material called grit stone.

Images and Symbolism

Emily Brontë's poetic vision is evident in the imagery used throughout Wuthering Heights. Metaphors of nature and the animal kingdom are pervasive. For example, the first Catherine describes Heathcliff to Isabella as "an arid wilderness of furze and whinstone," and as Catherine lies dying, Heathcliff foams "like a mad dog." References to weather are everywhere. A violent storm blows up the night Mr. Earnshaw dies; rain pours down the night Heathcliff runs off to London and again the night of his death. There are many scenes of raw violence, such as the bulldog attacking Catherine and Isabella crushing her wedding ring with a poker. The supernatural is evoked in the many references to Heathcliff as diabolical (literally, "like the devil") and the descriptions of the ghost of the first Catherine Linton. David Daiches points out in his introduction to *Wuthering Heights* that the references to food and fire, and to what he calls domestic routine, help "to steady" the story and to give credibility to the passion.

Structure

One of the major strengths of Wuthering Heights is its formal organization. The design of the time structure has significance both for its use of two narrators and because it allows the significant events in the novel to be dated precisely, though dates are almost never given explicitly. The triangular relationship that existed between Heathcliff, Catherine, and Edgar is repeated in Heathcliff's efforts to force young Catherine to marry Linton, though its resolution is ultimately different. On his arrival at Wuthering Heights, Lockwood sees the names "Catherine Earnshaw, Catherine Linton, Catherine Heathcliff scratched into the windowsill. In marrying Hareton, young Catherine Heathcliff will in turn become Catherine Earnshaw, thus completing the circle.

Historical Context

The Victorian Age (1837-1901)

England under the reign of Queen Victoria was in a prolonged phase of expansion. The Industrial Revolution saw the transformation of a predominately agricultural economy to a factory economy. Millions would eventually flock to London in search of the new jobs, but Emily Brontë grew up in the last days of rural England. The tenor of the times was conservative, and sensitive to society's unwillingness to accept women as authors, Emily, Charlotte, and Anne Brontë all published under male pseudonyms.

The tempestuous climate of northern England in Haworth, Yorkshire, left its mark on the Brontë children, whose fascination with the expanse and storms of the moors is emphasized in the novel. For Emily, who was never happy far from home, the local moorland and valleys, and the grit stone architecture typical of the age were the basis for the setting of *Wuthering Heights.*

Another influence on Brontë's writing was the folklore of the Yorkshire community. Tabitha Ackroyd, a maid in the Brontë household, was a rich source of stories about fairies and ghosts. References to folk beliefs and rituals are scattered throughout *Wuthering Heights*, particularly with reference to the deathwatch traditional in Yorkshire, as when Edgar sits the entire night with Catherine's body after her death, or to rituals surrounding funerals such as "bidding," an invitation to accompany a body to the grave. Extending or withholding such an invitation gave some indication of the state of family relationships.

Illness, Death, and Funeral Customs

Owing to the unforgiving climate and poor heating, illness and death were common occurrences in Yorkshire at the time the novel was created. Ill partly as a result of his stay at Wuthering Heights, Lockwood laments, "Oh, these bleak winds, and bitter, northern skies, and impassable roads, and dilatory country surgeons!" Emily Brontë's older sisters Maria and Elizabeth died of tuberculosis before they were fifteen, and in *Wuthering Heights*, Edgar and Linton also die of wasting diseases. Maria Branwell's death when Emily was only three may be the inspiration for the many motherless children in *Wuthering Heights.*

A period of mourning was formally observed after the death of a family member. The appropriate period of mourning depended on whether the deceased was a close or distant relative. For example, a year's mourning was usually observed for a husband or wife, and a week for the death of a second cousin. In *Wuthering Heights* Nelly is "bid to get mourning"—that is, to lay out dark clothes—for Catherine, whose aunt Isabella has died.

Compare & Contrast

- **Late 1700s:** World economies are predominately agrarian.
  1847: England is in the midst of an Industrial Revolution whose effects will be felt worldwide. Workers flock to cities from the countryside.
  Today: World economies are increasingly linked in a "global community." Intercultural communication and cultural diversity in the so-called service economy are a direct result of advances in transportation and communications.

- **Late 1700s:** Life expectancy is short, owing to harsh living and working conditions. Death in childbirth is common.
  1847: Medical advances and improved public health and sanitation decrease maternal and infant mortality.
  Today: Though high-technology medicine offers solutions to many medical problems, heart disease and cancer remain major killers, there is no cure for AIDS, and many countries grapple with increasing costs of health care for aging populations.

- **Late 1700s:** Inheritance in England passes from the father to the first-born male. A procedure called "strict settlement" must be invoked to bypass inheritance laws.
  1847: Full legal and economic equality for women is first championed in the United States by Elizabeth Cady Stanton.
  Today: Women worldwide have the right to vote, except in a few Muslim countries. In the United States, while the Equal Rights Amendment failed to obtain ratification, women increasingly bring successful sexual discrimination and sexual harassment suits against employers.

As the children of a minister, the Brontës felt the influence of religion both at home and at school. A fire-and-brimstone instructor may have been Emily Brontë's inspiration for Joseph, who can barely speak a word that does not invoke hellfire. Critics also suspect that this influence is at the root of Lockwood's dream at the beginning of *Wuthering Heights*, in which he is forced to listen to the Reverend Jabes Branderham preach a sermon divided into 490 parts.

Literary Traditions and Romanticism

Whereas Charlotte Brontë's *Jane Eyre* won immediate acclaim, the wild passion and coarseness of *Wuthering Heights* baffled its readers. In an essay in *Reference Guide to English Literature*, Winifred Gerin attributes the failure of the novel to its theme of indestructibility of the spirit, which was a "subject ... far removed from the general run of Victorian fiction—it belonged, if anywhere, to the gothic tradition, still being followed by Mary Shelley with her *Valperga* (1823) in Emily Brontë's childhood."

The time in which the action of *Wuthering Heights* takes place, and its themes of nature and the individual, coincides with the Romantic Movement in Europe, a turning away from reason and intellect in favor of free and more mystical ideas, inspired in part by the French Revolutionary War of 1789.

Inheritance and Social Position

Social position and respectability in this period were directly tied to possession of property. A country house owned by landed gentry like the Earnshaws and the Lintons was known as a "seat," a broad term that included both the tangible assets (for instance, the house and land) and intangible assets (for instance, the family name and any hereditary titles) of the family that owned it. In *Wuthering Heights*, the first Catherine tells Nelly that she is marrying Edgar Linton because to marry Heathcliff would degrade her (they would be beggars) and because she plans to use Linton's money to help Heathcliff to rise.

Seats passed from father to first-born male or to the next closest male relative if there were no sons in a family. The only way around this process was to invoke a device called "strict settlement," in force between 1650 and 1880, which allowed a father to dispose of his holdings as he liked through a trustee. Because Edgar Linton dies before ensuring that his daughter Catherine will inherit Thrushcross Grange, the land passes first to her husband, Linton, and after Linton's death to his father, Heathcliff.

In contrast to earlier times when incest was forbidden by law, in eighteenth-century England marriage between first cousins was looked upon favorably as a way of preserving position and property. A typical union was one of a woman who married her father's brother's son, which kept the seat of the bride's family under their control. In *Wuthering Heights*, in a perverse twist, the second Catherine Linton marries her father's sister's son, and in the absence of a strict settlement ends up losing her family's seat.

Landholding families typically maintained a large staff of servants who fulfilled the functions (for a man) of steward, valet, butler, and gardener, or (for a woman) of lady's maid, housekeeper, cook, and nurse. In a household the size of Wuthering Heights, whose inhabitants did not entertain, combining functions made economic sense. In the novel Joseph serves as both valet and steward, and Ellen as housekeeper, though her duties are fairly broadly defined.

Critical Overview

Initial reception to the publication of *Wuthering Heights* in 1847 was overwhelmingly negative. Published in a volume that also included her sister Anne Brontë's first novel, *Agnes Grey*, Emily's brooding tale managed to find favor only with Sydney Dobell and Algernon Charles Swinburne. "I have just read over *Wuthering Heights*," wrote Charlotte Brontë in her preface to the 1850 edition of her sister's book, "and, for the first time, have obtained a clear glimpse of what are termed (and, perhaps, really are) its faults.... *Wuthering Heights* must appear a rude and strange production ... in a great measure unintelligible, and —where intelligible—repulsive." The preface was intended as a defense of the writer and the work and must have achieved its aim, for the second edition of the novel was received more favorably. Algernon Charles Swinburne, writing in *The Athenaeum* in 1883, admitted to the awkward construction and clumsy method of narration "which no reader ... can undertake to deny," although these were minor faults. He was more troubled by "the savage note or the sickly symptom of a morbid ferocity," but was overall so impressed by the "special and distinctive character of its passion" that "it is certain that those who do like it will like nothing very much better in the whole world of poetry or prose."

A monograph by Charles Percy Sanger published in 1926 marked a major turning point in critical appreciation of the sophistication and complexity of the writing in *Wuthering Heights*, and today the novel is indisputably considered a work of genius. That critics cannot agree whether the book falls more neatly into the Gothic or Romantic literary tradition is accepted as further evidence of the work's uniqueness. In his introduction to the novel, David Daiches argues that the central question of *Wuthering Heights* is "Who and what is Heathcliff?", a question Daiches argues can be answered only by looking at the effect Heathcliff has on those around him. While Daiches agrees with the conventional view that the relationship between Heathcliff and the first Catherine is "curiously" sexless, he does find persuasive Thomas Moser's (1962) case for recurring sexual symbolism in the novel. Daiches echoes other critics in praising the book's narrative structure and other elements of its organization. He places special emphasis on the details of everyday living, and descriptions of food and hearth, that help to anchor the story and to make it believable. "One of Emily Brontë's most extraordinary achievements in this novel is the domiciling of the monstrous in the ordinary rhythms of life and work, thereby making it at the same time less monstrous and more disturbing." Tom Winnifrith, in the *Dictionary of Literary Biography*, picks up on the idea of Heathcliff as a force of nature and attributes his attraction in part to his association with the landscape and to his honesty, however brutal. This last idea highlights one of many ambiguities of the novel, a strength often commented on by scholars and critics. "Brontë's defiance of rigid categories and her refusal to divide people into saints and sinners," says Winnifrith, "is very un-Victorian.… Heathcliff's cruelty and Cathy's selfishness do not prevent them from being attractive. The Lintons are spoiled and weak, but Isabella's and her son's sufferings and Edgar's devotion to his wife win them sympathy." Winnifrith dismisses the oft-cited effort to fit the novel into an overall framework of storm and calm —that is, storm and calm opposed in the persons of Catherine and Heathcliff, but fused in the union of Catherine and Hareton—proposed by Lord David Cecil in *Early Victorian Novelists* (1934) as too schematic. He argues that some modern sociological interpretations ignore the book's enigmatic ending. Other modern critical articles on the novel, he says, "tend to be eccentric or to deal with only a very small section of the book." In an essay in *Reference Guide to English Literature*, Winifred Gerin describes the message of "the indissoluble nature of earthly love" as "profoundly metaphysical," its original failure easily explained by its gothic atmosphere, no longer in fashion at the time of publication. Gerin attributes the novel's "curious and lasting appeal" to the "unflagging excitement of the plot; the wild moorland setting; [and] … the originality of the characters." She calls Heathcliff's self-induced death by starvation "one of the most powerful and daring climaxes in English fiction."

"Whether it is right or advisable to create things like Heathcliff, I do not know," wrote Charlotte Brontë at the end of the preface to the 1850 edition. "I scarcely think it is. But this I know;

the writer who possesses the creative gift owns something of which he is not always master—something that at times strangely wills and works for itself." It is English literature's gain that Emily lost herself in her creation.

Sources

Charlotte Brontë, "Editor's Preface to the New [1850] Edition of Wuthering Heights," in *Wuthering Heights*, edited by David Daiches, Penguin, 1965, pp. 37-41.

David Daiches, editor, in the introduction to *Wuthering Heights*, Penguin, 1965, pp. 7-29.

Winifred Gerin, "Emily Brontë," in *Reference Guide to English Literature*, edited by D. L. Kirkpatrick, St. James Press, 1991, pp. 300-02.

Algernon Charles Swinburne, "Emily Brontë," in *The Athenaeum*, No. 2903, June 16, 1883, pp. 762-63.

Tom Winnifrith, "Emily Brontë," in *Dictionary of Literary Biography, Volume 21: Victorian Novelists before 1885*, edited by Ira B. Nadel and William E. Fredeman, Gale Research, 1983, pp. 55-67.

For Further Study

Miriam Allot, *The Brontës: The Critical Heritage*, Routledge, 1974.

> A collection of criticism on the works of the Brontë sisters, including reprints of early reviews of *Wuthering Heights* and *Poems by Currer, Ellis and Acton Bell* and Charlotte Brontë's observations on her sister's novel.

Terry Eagleton, "Myths of Power: A Marxist Study on *Wuthering Heights*" in *Case Studies In Contemporary Criticism: Wuthering Heights*, St. Martin's, 1992, pp. 399-414.

> Eagleton analyzes the novel in terms of class differences in nineteenth-century England.

Winifred Gerin, *Emily Brontë: A Biography*, Clarendon, 1971.

> Gerin discusses Emily Brontë's life and the effect of her environment on her work.

Philip K. Wion, "The Absent Mother in *Wuthering Heights*" in *American Imago*, Vol. 42, No. 2, 1985.

> Wion suggests that the early death of Emily Brontë's mother accounts for Brontë's portrayal of orphaned

characters in search of mother figures.